WHO IS HE?

Unveiling Truth in a World Full of Deception

TALLI LOPEZ

Trilogy Christian Publishers
A Wholly Owned Subsidiary of Trinity Broadcasting Network
2442 Michelle Drive
Tustin, CA 92780
Copyright © 2024 by Talli Lopez
All Scripture quotations, unless otherwise noted, taken from THE HOLY BIBLE, NEW INTERNATIONAL VERSION®, NIV® Copyright © 1973, 1978, 1984, 2011 by Biblica, Inc.® Used by permission. All rights reserved worldwide.
Scripture quotations marked (KJV) taken from *The Holy Bible, King James Version*. Cambridge Edition: 1769.
All rights reserved, including the right to reproduce this book or portions thereof in any form whatsoever.
For information, address Trilogy Christian Publishing
Rights Department, 2442 Michelle Drive, Tustin, CA 92780.
Trilogy Christian Publishing/ TBN and colophon are trademarks of Trinity Broadcasting Network.
For information about special discounts for bulk purchases, please contact Trilogy Christian Publishing.

Trilogy Disclaimer: The views and content expressed in this book are those of the author and may not necessarily reflect the views and doctrine of Trilogy Christian Publishing or the Trinity Broadcasting Network.

10 9 8 7 6 5 4 3 2 1
Library of Congress Cataloging-in-Publication Data is available.
ISBN 979-8-89597-110-9
ISBN 979-8-89597-111-6 (ebook)

DEDICATION

This book is dedicated to you, the reader. Perhaps you have been looking for what is true in a world full of theory. Maybe you are holding this book now, anticipating how you are going to disagree and find fault in its content. Maybe you are hoping to find an anchor of some sort. Whatever the reason is, I am so thankful for you. I pray that the Word in this book breaks ground in your heart, that you will allow yourself to receive what Jesus paid for you to have, that you will know how much He loves you. But most of all, my hope is that you go deeper in seeking Him, that you not take my word for it but that you come to the knowledge of truth and come to know Jesus for yourself. He is before all things, and in Him all things hold together. If something is missing in your life, I promise you, it can only be found in Him.

TABLE OF CONTENTS

Part 1: Who Is He? 9

Part 2: What Are We Forgiven From?. 23

Part 3: What about Grace? 57

PART 1
WHO IS HE?

Have you ever thought about what it means to be a false witness or bear false witness? Is there a difference between ideology and what is true? In this book, we are going to tap into scripture to see exactly what it means to be a Christian, what Jesus actually paid for us to have, and who Jesus is. It is no secret that people all over the world have fought about who Jesus is since the beginning of time. Some claimed him to be demon possessed, some knew him as a carpenter's son, some thought him to be the promised Messiah and even the Son of God. But what about you? Who do you say Jesus is? Can someone really come to know Jesus?

It was the Pharisees and Sadducees who did not believe Jesus to be the Messiah. They didn't believe Jesus to follow the Law. They knew theology but had no revelation. Believing themselves to be acceptable by their own efforts to know and follow the Law, they watched Jesus only to try and prove that he was a false prophet. Never coming to know him as truth, they remained bound to oppression. If someone never comes to know what is true, they will never possess discernment to know what is false. Ignorance will always be a breeding ground for fear. Fear creates oppression. Actually, oppression is simply to be controlled by fear. Fear is a spirit. The only thing that can get rid of fear is love. There is no fear in love, but perfect love drives out all fear, because fear has to do with punishment (1 John 4:18, NIV). Where does love come from? 1 John 4:8 tells us God is love. And John 14:6 tells us there is only one way to the Father, and that is through Jesus. But what does that actually mean? Many people believe Jesus to be good and kind. So they try to do good and be kind everywhere they go in an attempt to be like Jesus. They hear that Jesus ate with sinners but never want to acknowledge that he set those sinners free. When he told the woman caught in adultery that he didn't condemn her, he also told her to go and sin no more. When Jesus left the ninety-nine to get the one, he did not go join the one that was lost. He brought him back to shepherd him along with the ninety-nine. Jesus says in Luke 19:10, "For the Son of Man came to seek and save that which was lost." It was the image of God in man that was lost. Image can be defined as a representation of the external form of a person. Similar words are likeness or depiction. Colossians 1:15 tells us, "The Son is the image of the invisible God, the firstborn over all creation." Jesus knew God as his Father, and he knew himself as God's Son. He lived on the earth to carry out the will of his Father. Christ did not take on himself the glory of becoming high priest, but God said to him, "You are my Son and today I have become your Father" (Hebrews 5:5). During Jesus life on earth, he offered up prayers and petitions with fervent cries and tears to the one who could save him from death, and he was heard through his reverent submission. Son though he was, he learned obedience through what he suffered, and once made perfect, he became the source of eternal salvation for all who obey him and was designated

WHO IS HE?

by God to be high priest in the order of Melchizedek (Hebrews 5:7-10).

We know from 1 John 4:17 that as Jesus is, so are we in this world. So I ask again, who do you say Jesus is? A witness is someone who has seen something take place. A witness holds evidence and proof of something. Acts 1:8 declares that "we receive power when the Holy Spirit comes on us and we will be his witnesses in Jerusalem and all of Judea and Samaria, and to the ends of the earth." Have you received his glorious power? What have you witnessed about the Son of the living God? Let's look at scripture together and go deeper. Let's not take everyone else's word for it; let's come to know him ourselves.

There is an odd ideology that even though Jesus came to save us, we will still continue sinning and being sinners until we make heaven. It seems that not many people know what they have actually been saved from or what salvation even means. Many people believe that salvation means going to heaven and that eternal life is to live forever. John 17:3 tells us what eternal life is. It says, "And this is eternal life that they may know you, the only true God, and Jesus Christ whom you have sent." Eternal life is knowing Him. Please don't misunderstand me. I am in no way saying that we aren't going to heaven, and I am not saying that we won't live forever. But what I am saying is that eternal life is knowing the Father through the Son. Any other belief has simply come forth from false witnesses who claim to know

God, but their hearts are far from him. Jesus didn't come to show us how to do our best. He came to take us back to our Father. He did not come to make us good people or better people. He came to give us resurrection life, and it's not because we are good. In fact, in Mark 10:18 Jesus asks, "Why do you call me good?" Then Jesus answers his own question saying, "No one is good except God alone." In the context of this scripture, if you look it up, the man said to Jesus, "Good teacher, what must I do to have eternal life?" That's when Jesus asked why he calls Him good and tells Him no one is good except God alone. Jesus told him, "You know the commandments: 'You shall not murder, you shall not commit adultery, you shall not steal, you shall not give false testimony, you shall not defraud, honor your mother and your father." "Teacher," he declared, "all these things I have kept since I was a boy." Jesus looked at him and loved him. "One thing you lack, go and sell all your possessions and give to the poor, and you will have treasure in heaven. Then come follow me." The man went away saddened because he had great wealth. Jesus then told the disciples that man cannot save himself; it is impossible. But all things are possible with God. Salvation can only come through Jesus, the Son of God. But what actually is salvation?

We were born separated from God; because Adam sinned, we all died. We became cut off from God and became void and empty of the very purpose he designed us for. Mankind was reduced down to a restless wanderer on the earth. We see that God gave us the ten commandments so that we could once again have that which was lost. But man's hearts were hardened. Man had no understanding. Man thought if they just follow the law, then God would accept them. It has never been about God accepting man— it's always been about man accepting Jesus, God's One and Only Son. Everything that God created, he saw that it was good. But when man fell, man could no longer see God's goodness. God predestined us in Christ before the foundation of the world. And people have been fighting and arguing who that Jesus is, since the beginning of time. The Sadducees didn't believe in the Resurrection from the dead, and the Pharisees did not believe Jesus to be God's Son, because they knew him as Joseph's Son. They accused him of blasphemy. Their whole goal in life was to kill Jesus, the Son of God, who is the Son of Man—man, the one created in the image of God. They wanted to convince everyone that Jesus was just a good man who went around doing good. They did not acknowledge or believe him to be the one who came to set them free. Though they knew the Law, they were unbelievers in Jesus Christ. They thought they were good because they followed the Law, and they used all their time trying to trick Jesus to disagreeing with the Law or trick him to believe that he wasn't the Son of God. Even Satan himself tried to get Jesus to believe that he wasn't the Son of God. The religious people who wanted Jesus crucified were not the people who followed

WHO IS HE?

him. They were the people who did not believe that he was the Messiah, Son of the living God. They were trying to prove that he was just a man and even a false prophet. They had no understanding, no revelation of who Jesus is. They refused to come to know him and refused to go to him to have life. They didn't think they needed a Savior because they thought they were good all by themselves. They called themselves good and got along with everyone except Jesus. They denied Jesus to be the Christ. They thought that, because Jesus healed on the Sabbath, he was possessed by a demon. The leaders thought if they followed the commands, that is what made them good. But little did they know that, if you miss one of the 613 laws, you miss them all. Jesus fulfilled all of them. And he died to put his life in you, starting with his death. When he died, we died. When he rose, we rose with him. He came to take away the sins of the world. He didn't come to affirm the sinner. He didn't come to celebrate the sinner. He didn't come to condone the sinner. He also didn't come to condemn the sinner. But God sent his Son fully God and fully man, here, to the world to save the world through him! Why? Because the world needed a savior—whoever acknowledges their need for salvation and agrees that Jesus is the Son of God is a believer. The Law was not sent to be our Savior. The Law came to show man that he fell short of the glory of God. But the Law was powerless because it was weakened by mortal flesh. So God sent his own Son in the likeness of sinful flesh to be a sin offering, and he condemned sin in the flesh in order that the righteous requirement of the Law might be fully met in us, who do not live according to the flesh, but according to the Spirit. Those who live according to their flesh have their mind set on things that the flesh desires; but those who live by the Spirit have their mind set on what the Spirit desires (Romans 8:). Who is the Spirit? 2 Corinthians 3:18 says the Lord is Spirit. We know where the Spirit of the Lord is there is freedom. God sent his Son to again give us life in him because, without him, we remain dead in our sin, trying to be good people, all because we never truly got to know who Jesus Christ is.

For gifts and callings of God are without repentance (Romans 11:29, KJV) We can heal the sick, we can go to church, we can be nice to people, but at the end of the day, all that matters is: Did we come to know him to have life? When we turn to the Lord, the true Christ, the veil is taken away. This means our understanding is no longer darkened. When we turn to Christ, he lifts up our veil, and we see him face to face. Does this remind you of anything? I am talking to the bride of Christ.

> *Revelation 19:7-9: "Let us be glad and rejoice and give honor to him; for the marriage of the Lamb is come, and his wife has made herself ready. Fine linen, bright and clean was given her to wear."*

Isaiah 54:5: "For thy Maker is thy husband; the LORD of Hosts is his name and thy Redeemer the Holy One of Israel; the God of the whole earth shall he be called."

Ephesians 4:17: "So I tell you this, and insist on it in the Lord, that you must no longer live as the Gentiles do, in the uselessness of their thinking. They are darkened in their understanding and separated from the life of God because of the ignorance that is in them due to the hardening of heart. Having lost all sensitivity, they have given themselves over to the enjoyment of pleasure so as to indulge in every kind of impurity, and they are full of greed. That however is not the way of life you have learned when you heard about Christ and were taught in him in accordance with the truth that is in Jesus. You were taught with regard to your former way of life, to put off your old self, which is being corrupted by its deceitful desires; to be made new in the attitude of your minds and to put on the new self, created to be like God in true righteousness and holiness. Therefore each of you must put off falsehood and speak truthfully to your neighbor for we are all members of one body."

Stop right there. What does it mean, "We are all members

of one body"? Well, look at Colossians 1:17: "He is before all things and in him all things hold together. He is the head of the body- the body is the church; He is the beginning and the first born from among the dead, so that in everything he might have supremacy. For God was pleased to have all his fulness dwell in him, and through him, to reconcile to himself all things whether things on earth or on heaven, by making peace through his blood shed on the cross. Once you were alienated from God and were enemies in your minds because of your evil behavior. But now he has restored relationship with you by Christ's physical body through death to present you holy in his sight, without blemish, free from accusation-if you continue in your faith, established and firm, and do not move from the hope held out in the gospel."

Notice it says, "If you continue in your faith." Faith is the substance of our hope. Who is our hope? Christ in us! If you receive him, He is in you. And as you come to know Him, He will be revealed in you. As you come to the knowledge of truth, you will be made aware that He is with you. Even now until the ends of the earth, He will be with you.

Christ Jesus who died—more than that, who was raised to life—is at the right hand of God and is also interceding for us. Who shall separate us from the love of Christ? Shall trouble or hardship or persecution or famine or nakedness or danger or sword? As it is written: "For your sake we seek death all day long; we are more than conquerors through him who loved us. For I am convinced that neither death nor life, neither angels nor demons, neither the present nor the future, nor any powers, neither height nor depth, nor anything else in all creation will be able to separate us from the love of God that is in Christ" (Romans 8:35). The love of God can only be found in his Son. If we reject his Son, we are separated from the love of God because God's love is in his Son. Every promise in scripture is for the believer, not the unbeliever. The unbeliever can never have what God has promised until they come to the knowledge of truth and believe. Jesus gives us warning in John 8:24. He says, "I told you that you would die in your sins if you do not believe that I am he, you will indeed die in your sins." "Who are you," they asked. "Just what I've been telling you from the beginning," Jesus replied. "I have much to say in judgment of you. But he who sent me is trustworthy, and what I have heard from him I tell the world." They did not understand that he was telling them about his Father. So Jesus said, "When you have lifted up the Son of Man, then you will know that I am he and I do nothing on my own but speak just what the Father taught me, The one who sent me is with me; he has not left me alone, for I always do what pleases him." Even as he spoke, many believed him. To the Jews who had believed him, Jesus said, "If you hold to my teaching, you are really my disciples. Then you will know the truth and the truth will set you free." Freedom is not doing whatever you want. It is only in Christ that man will ever have true freedom. It is in Christ that we are children of God through faith, for all of us who have been baptized into Christ have clothed ourselves with Christ. It is for freedom that Christ set us free. Don't you know that all of us who were baptized into Christ Jesus were baptized into his death? We were therefore buried with him through baptism of death in order that, just as Christ was raised from the dead through the glory of the Father, we too may live a new life. It is Jesus who makes all things new. Jesus came to give us new life. Anyone who does not receive this new life in Christ is still under the curse of the Law of sin and death.

Galatians 3:13 says, "Christ redeemed us from the curse of the Law by becoming a curse for us, for it is written, 'cursed is everyone who is hung on a pole.' He redeemed us in order that the blessing given to Abraham might come to the Gentiles through Christ Jesus, so that by faith we might receive the promise of the Spirit." Everything God promised us is in Christ. Everyone who calls upon his name shall be saved. The power of God brings salvation to the believer. Through Jesus, we receive grace that calls us to obedience that comes from faith for his name's sake. We are called to belong to Jesus Christ. Redemption comes through Jesus. Obedience comes through Jesus. Revelation comes through Jesus Christ. Everything God gave us is in Christ. And God gave us a choice to accept Christ or reject Christ. But first he gave us his Word so we can come to know Christ. Then we can decide; we can choose to receive him or deny him. If you want to come to know him, just tell him. Ask him who he is. Ask him to show you. He will! Then when you truly come to know him, you can choose for yourself whom you will serve. Don't give up! Keep going until you meet him. You'll know when you do, because your life will never be the same.

PART 2

WHAT ARE WE FORGIVEN FROM?

WHAT ARE WE FORGIVEN FROM?

Now let's talk about sin. Here is the issue about accepting sin or even not calling sin "sin" or passing sin off as not your business. Everyone is born under the curse of the law, and the whole world is accountable to God. Therefore no one is declared righteous in God's sight by the works of the law; rather through the law we become conscious of our sin (Romans 3:20). The Law was never given to man with the intent for man to follow the law and become good. The Law was given so man would understand how far mankind had fallen short of the image of God. Please understand that, before the foundations of the earth, Jesus, the Lamb of God, was slain. God gave up His only Son to become sin for us. God made him who had no sin to be sin for us so that in him we might become the righteousness of God (2 Corinthians 5:21). Think about this. Jesus did not know sin. The Son of God did not know sin. Then he himself became sin, that we might become the righteousness of God through him.

We did not know sin until sin was revealed to us in the law. Once we are made aware of the law, we become aware that we are guilty of sin because we all sinned and fell short of God's glory. The payment for sin is death. That is the penalty. Here is where it gets tricky. The church at large has been taught to follow the law in hopes that will make them good and will get them into heaven. Some have even taught, if you are not good, that you are doomed to hell. If you aren't the means of your own salvation, then it is not your actions that will ever determine your destiny. However, your actions are determined by your belief. If your belief is in yourself and not Jesus, you will continue trying hard and falling short every time. But if your belief is in Jesus, He will become your salvation. The church has believed that Jesus died so we could go to heaven someday and have life after we die. But here is the thing: Scripture actually says that salvation is for today (2 Corinthians 6:2). We were born dead in Adam. That death is the penalty of sin. It is what we were born into. And we can only be made alive in Christ (1 Corinthians 15:22). Following the law does not bring us salvation. The Bible says that Jesus is the only way to the Father, the one we were separated from in the beginning because of the fall of man. But I'm learning that so many people believe life is just about doing good and being nice to people. If they do a couple of good deeds, then that probably cancels out their bad ones, and somehow that is all they need to clear their conscience. But if we blindly believe that, we will never truly be free. We will only be as good as we are doing, living to please ourselves and to make ourselves look good. People are so caught up defending sin and hiding sin because of shame. Being sin-conscious is not freedom from sin. Jesus does not give us freedom to sin. He gives us freedom from sin. When we come to know Jesus, we are able to receive this gift of life from him. Jesus bought us from death—he redeemed us from the curse of the Law (Galatians 3:13). We were born into death. Jesus bought us from death. Now we belong to

WHAT ARE WE FORGIVEN FROM?

him, not so we can continue on in our old life ignorant of truth but so that we can have a new life in him.

So we now know that death came through one man, Adam. And life comes through one man, Jesus! Salvation is not about being good. Does good come from salvation? Of course! But Jesus did not come to make you good. He came to give you life because you were born dead in Adam. I will say that again. Jesus did not come to make you good; He came to bring you life. There is no way to have life apart from Jesus. Without him we are under the curse of the law. When someone is under the curse of the law, death is their authority and ruler. The sting of death is sin, and the power of sin is the law (1 Corinthians 15:56). No matter how hard they try or desire to do what is right, they can't, because they are a slave to sin. Sin is a product of unbelief. Sin is cursed in the flesh. So when a person lives according to their own will and not God's, they remain in the flesh. The one who sows to please his sinful nature will reap destruction (Galatians 6:8). The flesh will have you trying to be a good person in hopes that is what "qualifies" you or justifies you. Galatians 6:12 tells us that there will be people who want to impress by means of the flesh; they will try to get you to follow the law so that they will not be persecuted for the cross of Christ. They want to boast about what they have done in the flesh. But we know the flesh counts for nothing; what counts is the new creation. This new life is only found in Christ. No one is justified by the works of the law; we are only justified by faith in the finished works of Jesus. This faith does not nullify the law; it is through faith that we uphold the law. Jesus redeems us from the curse of the law, not so that we can continue on in sin but that, through faith, we uphold the law. Redemption is to be saved from sin and the action of gaining or regaining possession of something or clearing a debt. The grace that we are justified by comes through the action of Jesus clearing our debt and him gaining possession of us. He is the one who saves us from death, the death we were born into because of the fall of man. When man fell, we all fell. Death entered through that one man. So Jesus became the sacrifice—God presented Jesus as a sacrifice of atonement, through the shedding of his blood—to be received by faith. Jesus was delivered over to death for our sins and raised to life for our justification. Our justification is in his life, his resurrection life. Therefore, since we have been justified through faith, we have peace with God through our Lord, Jesus Christ, through whom we gained access by faith into this grace in which we now stand. And we boast in the hope of the glory of God.

So grace actually comes through faith. The peace we now have with God comes through Jesus Christ being our Lord. "Lord" is someone who has authority, such as a master to a servant. Meaning, we are now in submission to Christ being our head, Christ being our authority that brings us peace with God. We are saved by grace through faith (Ephesians 2:8). Look at 2 Corinthians 6:1: "As God's co-workers we urge you not to receive God's grace in vain, for he says in the time of my favor I heard you, and in the day of salvation I helped you. I tell you, now is the time of God's favor, now is the day of salvation." God has spoken to us and has opened wide his heart to us through his Son. He has not withheld his affection from us, but, rather, we have withheld ours from him.

Christ died for us while we were sinners. We are now justified by his blood—how much more shall we be saved from God's wrath through him! For if while we were enemies, we were reconciled to him through the death of his Son, how much more, having reconciled, shall we be saved through his life! Not only is this so but we also boast in God through our Lord Jesus Christ, through whom we now have received reconciliation. To reconcile is to restore relation and to connect. We are connected to him by his death, and when He rose, we also rose. The law charged sin against our account. The law demanded a price and accused us of breaking the law. We had a debt because we could not hold up our agreement. Jesus paid that debt, purchased us from death, and now in him, we who once were far away have been brought near by the blood of Christ. For he himself is our peace who has made the two groups one and has destroyed the barrier, the dividing wall of hostility, by setting aside in his flesh the law with its commands and regulations. His purpose was to create in himself one new humanity out of the two, making peace, and in one body to reconcile both of them to God through the cross, by which he put to death their hostility. He came and preached peace to you who were far away and peace to those who were near. For through him we both have access to the Father by one Spirit. Consequently, you are no longer foreigners and strangers but fellow citizens with God's people and also members of his household built on the foundation of the apostles and prophets with Christ Jesus himself as their cornerstone. In him, the whole building is joined together and rises to become a holy temple in the Lord. And in him, you too are being built together to become a dwelling place in which God lives by his Spirit. Let's read Ephesians 3:6: "The mystery is that through the gospel the Gentiles are heirs together with Israel, members of one body and sharers together in the promise of Jesus Christ." The mystery was kept hidden in God for ages past. His intent was that through the church the manifold wisdom of God should be made known to the rulers and authorities in the heavenly realms according to his eternal purpose that he accomplished in Christ Jesus our Lord. In him and through him, we may approach God with freedom and confidence. This is not man's interpretation; the mystery of God has been revealed through the Spirit. This is why it is imperative that we spend time with the Lord and sow to please the Spirit. This mystery, now made know to us by revelation, comes from the substance of our hope. What is that hope? It is Christ in us! Revelation is the unveiling, the revealing of Jesus Christ that God gives to his servants—Jesus being the head and the Church being the body, joined together, a new glorified body all for the eternal purpose of his great name!

Philippians 3:15-20 says, "All of us, who are mature should take such a view of things. And if on some point you think differently, that too God will make clear to you. Only let us live up to what we already attained. Join together in following my example, brothers and sisters, and just as you have us a model, keep your eyes on those who live as we do. For, as I have often told you before and now tell you again even with tears, many live as enemies of the cross of Christ. Their destiny is destruction and their god is their stomach, and their glory is in their shame. Their mind is set on earthly things. But our citizenship is in heaven and we eagerly await a Savior from there, the Lord Jesus Christ, who, by the power that enables him to bring everything under his control, will transform our lowly bodies so that they will be like his glorious body."

And again, Ephesians 2:19 says, "consequently, you are no longer foreigners and strangers, but fellow citizens with God's people and also many members of his household, built on the foundation of the apostles and prophets, with Christ Jesus himself as the chief cornerstone. In him the whole building is joined together and rises to become a holy temple in the Lord. And in him you too are being built together to become a dwelling in which God lives by his

Spirit."

Colossians 3:1 says, "Since then, you have been raised with Christ, set your minds on things above, not on earthly things. For you died and your life is now hidden with Christ in God. When Christ, who is your life, appears, you will appear with him in glory." Appear means made visible. Look at 1 Corinthians 1:7: "Therefore you do not lack any spiritual gift as you eagerly await for our Lord Jesus Christ to be revealed. He will also keep you firm to the end, so that you will be blameless on the day of our Lord Jesus Christ, God is faithful, who has called you into fellowship with his Son, Jesus our Lord." Now let's go back to Philippians 3 where scripture says many live as enemies of the cross of Christ. Their mind is set on earthly things, but our citizenship is in heaven. Citizenship is a position or status of being legally recognized. People who live as enemies of the cross have their mind positioned on things of the earth, but our position is that we are legal residents of heaven. It says, "We await a Savior from there; the Lord Jesus Christ, who by the power that enables him to bring everything under his control, will transform our lowly bodies so that they will be like his glorious body." Lowly is a position. What is the lowly position? It is the fallen state of man. In man's fallen nature, he lives as an enemy of the cross. But we know our posture is heaven. What is heaven? Genesis 1:1 tells us, "In the beginning God created the heavens and the earth. Now the earth was formless and empty, darkness was over the surface of the deep and the Spirit was hovering over the waters." (Heaven is the Spirit of God) When God created the heavens and the earth, he created light. God saw that the light was good and he separated light from darkness. Now go to John 1: "In the beginning was the Word, and the Word was with God and the Word was God. He was in the beginning with God. All things were made through him and without him nothing was made, that has been made. In him was life, and that life was the light of men. The light shines in the darkness and darkness has never overcome it." We see in Genesis 1 that God made light out of darkness. In John 1, we see that in God who is his Word was life and that life was the light of men. John bore witness to this light; John wasn't the light, but he came to bear witness about this light. "The true light which gives light to everyone was coming into the world, and the world was made through him, yet the world did not know him. He came to his own but his own did not receive him. But to those who did receive him, who believed in his name, he gave the right to become children of God who were born, not of blood, nor of the will of man, but born of God. And the Word became flesh and dwelt among us and we have seen his glory, glory as of the only Son from the Father, full of grace and truth."

If the Spirit of God is our posture, then we who believe in the Name of Jesus and receive him, we become children of God born not of blood nor of the will of man but of

God. And the Word became flesh and dwelt among us. When we receive the Word, the Word becomes flesh and dwells among us. He who knew no sin became sin so that we might become the righteousness of God through him. 1 Corinthians 1:20 says, "Where is the wise person? Where is the teacher of the law? Where is the philosopher of this age? Has God not made foolish the wisdom of the world? For since in the wisdom of God the world through its wisdom did not know him, God was pleased through the foolishness of what was preached to save those who believe. Jews demand signs and Greeks look for wisdom, but we preach Christ crucified; a stumbling block to Jews and foolishness to Gentiles. But to whom God has called, both Jews and Greeks, Christ the power of God and the wisdom of God. For the foolishness of God is wiser than human wisdom and the weakness of God is stronger than human strength. Back up to verse eighteen. "For the message of the cross is foolishness to those who are perishing, but to us who are being saved it is the power of God. For it is written: 'I will destroy the wisdom of the wise; the intelligence of the intelligent I will frustrate.'"

Now look at Isaiah 29:13: "The LORD says, 'These people come near to me with their mouth and honor me with their lips, but their hearts are far from me. Their worship of me is based on merely human rules that they have been taught. Therefore once more I will astound these people with wonder upon wonder; the wisdom of the wise

WHAT ARE WE FORGIVEN FROM?

will perish, the intelligence of the intelligent will vanish. Woe to those who go into great depths to hide their plans from the Lord, who do their work in darkness and thinks who sees us? Who will know? You turn things upside down as if the potter were taught to be like the clay! Shall what is formed say to the one who formed it, you did not make me? Can the pot say to the potter, you know nothing?'"

God says, "The intelligence of the intelligent will vanish." Intelligence is the ability to acquire and apply knowledge and skill. The Lord says, "these people come to me with their mouth, honor me with their lips, but their hearts are far from me." How is this so? Human beings have the ability to acquire and apply knowledge and skill. This can be taught by mere humans. It does not require faith and does not connect us or restore us back to God as our Father. This is why it was the teachers of the Law who tried to trap Jesus and trick Jesus. They were relying on human wisdom from the knowledge they acquired for life application. Look back at 1 Corinthians 1:21: "For since in the wisdom of God the world through its wisdom did not know him, God was pleased through the foolishness of what was preached to save those who believe." We see here there is the wisdom of God, and there is worldly wisdom. Worldly wisdom does not know God. God was pleased through what was preached to save those who believe. What does he mean, foolishness? 1 Corinthians 1:26 says, "Brothers and sisters, think of what you were when you were called. Not many of you were wise by human standards, not many were influential; not many were of noble birth. But God chose the foolish things of the world to confound the wise; God chose the weak things of the world to shame the strong. God chose the lowly things of this world and the despised things - and the things that are not- to nullify the things that are, so that no one may boast before him. It is because of him that you are in Christ Jesus, who has become wisdom from God- that is our righteousness, holiness, and redemption. As it is written: "Let the one who boasts, boast in the Lord." Paul says, "My message and my preaching were not with wise and persuasive words, but with a demonstration of the Spirit's power so that your faith may not rest on human wisdom, but on God's power." Let's continue in 1 Corinthians 2:6, "We do however, speak a message of wisdom among the mature, but not the wisdom of this age or the rulers of this age, who are coming to nothing. No! We declare God's wisdom, a mystery that has been hidden and that God destined for our glory before time began. None of the rulers of this age understand it, for if they had they would have not crucified the Lord of glory. However, it is written: 'What no eye has seen, what no ear has heard, and what no human mind has conceived—the things God has prepared for those who love him'—these are the things God has revealed to us by his Spirit. The Spirit searches all things, even the deep things of God. For who knows a person's thoughts except their own spirit within them? In the same way no one knows the thoughts of God except the Spirit of God. What we have received is not the spirit of the world, but the Spirit who is from God, so that we may understand what God has freely given us. This is what we speak, not in words taught by human wisdom but in words taught by the Spirit, explaining spiritual realities with Spirit taught words. The person without the Spirit does not accept the things that come from the Spirit of God but considers them foolishness and cannot understand them because they are discerned only through the Spirit. The person with the Spirit makes judgements about all things, but such a person is not subject to merely human judgements, for, who has known the mind of the Lord so as to instruct him? But we have the mind of Christ!"

Scripture tells us there is a day that will come and test the quality of your work with fire. If what has been built survives, the builder will receive a reward. If it is burned up, the builder will suffer loss but will be saved, even though only one escaping through the flames. The foundation can be no other foundation other than the one already laid, which is Jesus Christ. Let's look at 1 Corinthians 3:18: "Do not deceive yourselves. If any of you think you are wise by the world's standards of this age, you should become fools so that you may become wise. For the wisdom of this world is foolishness in God's sight. As it is written: He catches the wise in their craftiness and again, the Lord knows that the thoughts of the wise are futile. So then no more boasting in human leaders! All things are yours, whether Paul or Apollos or Cephas or the world or life or death or the present or the future- all are yours, and you are of Christ, and Christ is of God." Proverbs 9:10: "The fear of the LORD is the beginning of wisdom, and knowledge of the holy One is understanding."

1 John 5:18: "We know anyone born of God does not continue to sin; the One who was born of God keeps them safe, and the evil one can not harm them. We know that we are children of God, and that the whole world is under the control of the evil one. We know also that the Son of God has come and has given us understanding, so that we may know him who is true. And we are in him who is true by being in his Son, Jesus Christ. He is the true God and eternal life. Dear children, keep yourselves from idols." The Son of God has come and given us understanding that we may know him who is true. Scripture says that he is the true God and eternal life. Jesus is the Son of God. He is not a slave of God. A slave has no permanent place in a family, but a son belongs to it forever. A slave is someone who is forced to work for and obey another. A slave is considered property valued at the worth of their work. But a son—a son is different than a slave. A slave is not free. But he who is a son is free. If you are oppressed by a master, you do not know the son. Because the son sets you free. Who the Son sets free is free indeed! Jesus is the manifest Word of God. We are his body. Now remember the Jews had not

WHAT ARE WE FORGIVEN FROM?

yet received Jesus as the Messiah. They were waiting for the Messiah. In John 8:33, they are having a conversation with Jesus. Jesus had said, "If you hold on to my teaching, you are really my disciples. Then you will know the truth and the truth will set you free." They answered him, "We are Abraham's descendants and have never been slaves of anyone, how can you say that we shall be set free?" Jesus replied, "Very truly I tell you everyone who sins is a slave to sin. Now a slave has no permanent place in a family but a son belongs to it forever. So if the Son sets you free you will be free indeed. I know that you are Abraham's descendants yet you are looking for a way to kill me, because you have no room in your heart for my Word. I am telling you what I have seen in the Father's presence, and you are doing what you have heard from your Father." "Abraham is our father," they answered. "If you were Abraham's children," Jesus said, "then you would do what Abraham did. As it is, you are looking for a way to kill me, a man who has told you the truth that I heard from God, Abraham did not do such things. You are doing the works of your own father." "We are not illegitimate children," they protested. "The only father we have is God himself." Jesus said to them, "If God were your father you would love me. Why is my language not clear to you? Because you are unable to hear what I say, you belong to your father the devil. You want to carry out his desires and kill me. He was a murderer from the beginning, not holding to the truth, for there is no truth in him. When he lies he speaks his native language, for he is a liar and the father of lies. Yet because I tell you the truth you do not believe me! Can anyone prove me guilty of sin? If I am telling the truth then why don't you believe me? Whoever belongs to God hears what God says. The reason you do not hear is because you do not belong to God." They go on to accuse Jesus that he is demon possessed. Jesus makes it known to them that he is only there to glorify God and not himself.

Now let's back up to where they told Jesus they were not illegitimate children and that the only father they had was God himself. In John 14:6, we hear Jesus say, "No one comes to the Father except through me." The Jews were trying to convince Jesus that God was their father, but because they did not have room for his Word and they were trying to kill him, Jesus tells them that God can't be their father because the only way to God the Father is through Jesus, his Son. They were trying to get rid of Jesus, the Son of God, the manifest Word of God. They had no room for truth. They had no room for the Word of God but still considered themselves to be children of God. Jesus told them that God was not their father because they rejected truth to believe they could be sons without receiving and believing Jesus to be the only way to the Father. Illegitimate means not authorized by law and not in accordance with accepted standard. Jesus is the only Son of God, and that is the standard. Look at Isaiah 59:19: "When the enemy comes in like a flood, the Spirit of the LORD raises the standard

WHAT ARE WE FORGIVEN FROM?

against him." The enemy is the one who opposes God's Word. An enemy can be anyone who is in the flesh and hostile to God. When he comes in like a flood, the Spirit of God raises the standard. Who is the standard? None other than Jesus Christ, the Son of the living God! Think about this. While we were sinners Christ died for us. Romans 6:4 says, "we are therefore buried with him through baptism into death in order that, just as Christ was raised from the dead through the glory of the Father, we too may live a new life. For we have been united with him in death like his, we will certainly also be united with him in a resurrection like his. For we know that our old self was crucified with him so that the body ruled by sin might be done away with, that we should no longer be slaves to sin—because anyone who has died has been set free from sin. For if we died with Christ, we believe that we will also live with him. For we know that since Christ was raised from the dead, He can not die again; death no longer has mastery over him. The death he died he died to sin once for all, but the life he lives he lives to God. In the same way recon yourselves dead to sin but alive to God in Christ Jesus. Therefore do not let sin reign in your mortal body so that you obey its evil desires. Do not offer any part of your body as an instrument of wickedness, but rather offer yourselves to God as those who have been brought from death to life, and offer every part of yourself to him as an instrument of righteousness. For sin shall no longer be your master because you are no longer under law but under grace." Grace sets us free from sin. Sin was our master. The death Jesus died, he died to sin, once for all (Romans 6:10). When he died, we died. When he rose, we rose. We have new life in him and only him. We are saved by grace (being set free from sin) through faith. Faith, being the substance of hope and hope being Christ in us.

Jesus says in John 10:39, "For judgment I have come into this world, so that the blind will see and that those who see will become blind. Pharisees who were with him heard him say this and asked, 'What? Are we blind to?' Jesus said, 'If you were blind, you would not be guilty of sin; but now you claim you can see, your guilt remains.'" A Pharisee is a member of ancient Jewish sect, distinguished by strict requirements of the Law claiming to be superior. In other words, Pharisees are people who believe themselves to be good because they do right. Back to John 10:1, (Jesus speaking) "Very truly I tell you Pharisees, anyone who does not enter the sheep pen by the gate but climbs in some other way, is a thief and a robber. The one who enters by the gate is the shepherd of the sheep. The gatekeeper opens the gate for him, and the sheep listen to his voice. He calls his own sheep by name and leads them out. When he has brought out all his own, he goes ahead of them and his sheep follow him because they know his voice. But they will never follow the voice of a stranger; in fact they will run away from him because they do not recognize his voice." Jesus used this figure of speech, but the Pharisees did not understand what he was telling them. Therefore Jesus said again, "Very truly

WHAT ARE WE FORGIVEN FROM?

I tell you, I am the gate for the sheep. All who have come before me are thieves and robbers, but the sheep have not listened to them. I am the gate; whoever enters through me will be saved. They will come and go and find pasture. The thief comes only to steal and kill and destroy; I have come that they may have life and life more abundant." A thief is someone who steals another person's property. Often when a thief breaks in to steal what does not belong to him, he will wear a mask of some sort. Scripture tells us that Satan himself masquerades as an angel of light. A masquerade is a false show or an attempt to make something that is not true appear true. Which takes us back to false witness, false apostles, and deceitful workers masquerading as apostles of Christ. A masquerade is not the same as faith. Faith is the substance of things hoped for, even when the evidence is not seen. Faith comes from believing in the finished work of Christ. Faith is agreeing with the Word of God and the promises of God. Faith comes by hearing the things of God through the Spirit of God. We are saved by being set free from sin and hearing the word of God. We are saved by grace through faith. Being set free from sin as our master is grace (Romans 6:14). But one who masquerades is one who is still a slave to sin, falsely pretending to know Jesus and believing him. Satan is crafty. And like him, false witnesses attempt to make themselves or their work to be good. Their only claim to Christ is that he was good and kind to everyone. So in their attempt to be like Christ, they walk the earth trying to be kind and do good. But in Mark

WHO IS HE?

10:18, Jesus asked, "Why do you call me good? No one is good except God alone." This cannot be repeated enough, Jesus did not come to make us good—He came to lead us to God, our Father, whom we were separated from in the beginning. It's not a formula of steps to be accepted. It's accepting that Jesus is the only Son of God and that the only way to the Father is through him. There are not many ways to God. There is one way! And his name is Jesus. The only way to God is through his Son; any other way makes you a thief and a robber. Which brings us back to John 10:10: "The thief comes to steal, kill and destroy but I have come that they may have life and have it abundantly. I am the good shepherd; I know my sheep and my sheep know me—just as the Father knows me and I know my Father. I lay my life down for the sheep. I have other sheep that are not of this sheep pen. I must bring them also. They too will listen to my voice, and there shall be one flock and one shepherd. The reason my Father loves me is that I lay down my life—only to take it up again. No one takes it from me but I lay it down of my own accord. I have the authority to lay it down and take it up again. This authority I learned from my Father." The Jews heard his words and were divided again. Many of them said, "He is demon possessed and raving mad. Why listen to him?" But others said, "These are not the sayings of a man possessed by a demon. Can a demon open the eyes of the blind?" Later on, in winter at the Festival of Dedication at Jerusalem, Jesus was in the temple courts. The Jews gathered around him

WHAT ARE WE FORGIVEN FROM?

saying, "How long will you keep us in suspense? If you are the Messiah, tell us plainly." Jesus answered, "I did tell you, but you do not believe. The works I do in my Fathers Name testify about me, but you do not believe because you are not my sheep. My sheep listen to my voice; I know them and they follow me. I give them eternal life and they shall never perish; no one will snatch them from my hand. My Father who has given them to me, is greater than all; no one can snatch them out of my Fathers hand, I and the Father are one." Again, the Jewish opponents picked up stones to stone him but Jesus said to them, "I have shown you many good works from the Father. For which of these works do you stone me?" "We are not stoning you for good works," they replied, "But for blasphemy because you a mere man claim to be God." Jesus answered them, "Is it not written in your law, 'I have called you gods?' If he called them gods to whom the Word of God came and scripture cannot be set aside—what about the One whom the Father set apart as his very own and sent into the world? Why then do you accuse me of blasphemy because I said I am God's Son? Do not believe me unless I do the works of my Father. But if I do them, even though you do not believe me, believe the works, that you may know and understand that the Father is in me and I am in the Father."

Go to John 14:10 where Jesus is speaking. "Don't you believe that I am in the Father and that the Father is in me? The Words I say to you I don't speak on my own authority.

WHO IS HE?

Rather it is the Father living in me who is doing the work. Believe me when I say I am in the Father and the Father is in me, or at least believe on the evidence of the work themselves. Very truly I tell you whoever believes in me will do the work I do and they will do even greater things than these because I am going to the Father. And I will do whatever you ask in my Name, so that the Father may be glorified in the Son, you may ask anything in my name and I will do it. If you love me, keep my commands. And I will ask the Father and he will give you another advocate to help you and be with you forever- The Spirit of Truth. The world cannot accept him or knows him, but you know him for he lives with you and will be in you. I will not leave you as orphans; I will come to you. Before long the world will not see me anymore, but you will see me. Because I live, you will also live. On that day you will realize that I am in my Father and you are in me, and I am in you. Whoever has my commands and keeps them is the one who loves me. The one who loves me will be loved by my Father, and I too will love them and show myself to them." Then Judas said, "But, Lord why do you intend to show yourself to us and not to the world?" Jesus replied, "Anyone who loves me will obey my teaching. My Father will love them and we will come and make our home with them. Anyone who does not love me will not obey my teaching. These words you hear are not my own; they belong to the Father who sent me. All this I have spoken with you. But the Advocate, the HOLY SPIRIT, whom the Father will send in my Name will teach you all things and remind you of everything I have said to you. Peace I leave with you; my peace I give you. I do not give to you as the world gives. Do not let your hearts be troubled, do not be afraid. You have heard me say I am going away and coming back to you. If you loved me you would be glad I am going to the Father, for the Father is greater than I. I have told you now before it happens, so that when it does happen, you will believe. I will not say much more to you, for the prince of this world is coming. He has no hold over me, but he comes so that the world may learn that I love my Father and do exactly what my Father has commanded me." Notice when Jesus says, "the prince of this world is coming." Now let's go to Ephesians 2: "As for you, you were dead in your transgressions and sins, in which you used to live when you followed the ways of the world and the prince and ruler of the kingdom of the air, the spirit who is now at work in the disobedient. All of us lived among them at one time, gratifying the cravings of our flesh and following its desires and thoughts. Like the rest, we were by nature deserving of his wrath. But because of his great love for us, God who is rich in mercy made us alive with Christ even when we were dead in sin-it is by grace you have been saved. And God raised us up with Christ and seated us with him in the heavenly realms in Christ Jesus, in order that in the coming ages he might show the incomparable riches of his grace, expressed in his kindness to us in Christ Jesus. For it is by grace you have been saved through faith—and this is not from yourselves, it is a gift of God- not by works so that no one may boast. For we are God's handiwork, created in Christ Jesus to do good works, which God prepared in advance for us to do."

We are created in Christ. Everything we've been promised and everything we've been given is in Christ. If we deny him, refuse to acknowledge the Word as truth, if we do not allow his Word to penetrate our heart, if his Word is not found in us, if we reject his teaching, then he is not in us, and we are apart from him. Apart from him we can do nothing. If we claim we have no sin and reject him to continue life in sin, we remain liars and the truth is not in us. If we refuse this grace as to be saved and try to save ourselves by being "good people," we will never come to the knowledge of truth as to be saved. Satan does not have the authority over you to keep you separated from God. But if you never come to the knowledge of God, you will believe a lie for the rest of your life. God said, "For as the heavens are higher than the earth, so are my ways higher than your ways and my thoughts higher than your thoughts." See, when man fell, he never got back up until God called him higher. But when God called him higher, man could still not get up because he was bound by the prince and power of the air. Jesus said, "The prince of this world is coming, he has no hold over me, but he comes that the world may know that I love my Father and do exactly what my Father has commanded." You see, the enemy will have you carrying out the desires of your flesh, forcing you

WHAT ARE WE FORGIVEN FROM?

to believe that is who you are and that God doesn't love you. Just like Eve believed the serpent when she ate the apple, he will have you feeding on the very thing that is killing you. And when you do, judgment will come on you. If you don't know truth, you will be deceived. You will hide because of condemnation that comes from unbelief. But Jesus did not come to condemn. He came to bring life. Man could not get to God. So God became a man, as Jesus, Son of man and Son of God. Jesus says in John 12:47, "If anyone hears my Words but does not keep them, I do not judge that person. For I did not come to judge the world but to save the world. There is a judge for the one who rejects me and does not accept my Words; the very Words I have spoken will condemn them at the last day. For I did not speak on my own, but the Father who sent me commanded me to say all that I have spoken. I know that his commands lead to eternal life. So whatever I say is just what the Father has told me to say." It is the Son who carries the judgment (John 5:22). Read Isaiah 52:13 and Isaiah 53:6. "See, my servant will act wisely, he will be lifted up and raised highly exalted. Just as there were many who were appalled at him, his appearance was so disfigured beyond that of any human being and his form marred beyond that of any human likeness—so he will sprinkle many nations, and kings will shut their mouths because of him. For what they were told, they will see, and what they have not heard they will understand. Who has believed our message and to whom has the arm of the LORD been revealed? He grew up before him like a tender shoot, and like a root out of the ground. He had no beauty or majesty to attract us to him, nothing in his appearance that we should desire him. He was despised and rejected by mankind, a man of suffering familiar with pain. Like one from whom people hide their face, he was despised and we held him in low esteem. Surely he took up our pain, and bore our suffering, yet we considered him punished by God, stricken by him and afflicted. But he was pierced for our transgressions, he was crushed for our iniquities, the punishment that brings us peace was upon him and by his wounds we are healed. We all like sheep have gone astray, each of us has turned our own way; and the LORD has laid on him the iniquity of us all."

Jesus says in John 12:30, "This was for your benefit not mine. Now is the time of judgment on this world; now the prince of this world will be driven out. And I, when I am lifted up from the earth, will draw all people to myself." He said this to show what kind of death he was going to die. The crowd spoke up. "We have heard from the Law that the Messiah will remain forever, so how can you say the Son of man must be lifted up? Who is the Son of man?" We know from Mark 8:31-35 that the son of man must suffer many things and be rejected by the elders, the chief priests and teachers of the law, that he must be killed and three days later raise again. Jesus spoke plainly about this, and Peter took him aside and began to rebuke him. But when Jesus turned and looked at his disciples, he looked at Peter and said, "Get the behind me, Satan. You do not have in mind the concerns of God, but merely human concerns. Whoever wants to be my disciple must deny themselves and take up their cross and follow me. For whoever wants to save their life will lose it, whoever loses their life for my sake will find it." What does it mean when Jesus says deny yourself, pick up your cross, and follow me? When Jesus carried his cross, he was led like a lamb to the slaughter (Isaiah 53:7-12), "and as a sheep before its shearers is silent, so he did not open his mouth. By oppression and judgment, he was taken away. Yet who of this generation protested? For he was cut off from the land of the living for the transgressions of my people he was punished. He was assigned a grave with the wicked, and with the rich in his death, though he had done no violence, nor was any deceit found in his mouth. Yet it was the Lord's will to crush him and cause him to suffer, and though the LORD makes his life an offering for sin, he will see his offspring and prolong his days, and the will of the LORD will prosper in his hand. After he has suffered, he will see the light of life and be satisfied; by his knowledge my righteous servant will justify many, and he will bear their iniquities. Therefore, I will give him a portion among the great, and he will divide the spoils with the strong, because he poured out his life unto death, and he was numbered with the transgressors, for he bore the sin of many, and made intercession for the transgressors."

Christ Jesus, being in very nature God (Philippians 2:6-11) "did not consider equality with God something to be used to his own advantage; rather, he made himself nothing by taking the very nature of a servant, being made in human likeness. And being found in appearance as a man, he humbled himself by becoming obedient to death— even death on a cross! Therefore, God exalted him to the highest place and gave him the name that is above every name, that at the name of Jesus every knee should bow, in heaven and on earth and under the earth, and every tongue acknowledge that Jesus Christ is Lord, to the glory of God the Father."

"Let us continue to work out our salvation with fear and trembling, for it is God who works in us to will and to act in order to fulfill his good purpose" (Philippians 2:13). "The patriarch David died and was buried, and his tomb is here to this day. But he was a prophet and knew that God had promised him on oath that he would place one of his descendants on his throne. Seeing of what was to come, he spoke of the resurrection of the Messiah, that he was not abandoned to the realm of the dead, nor did he let his body see decay. God has raised Jesus to life and we are all witnesses of it" (Acts 2:33-36). "Exalted to the right hand of God, he has received from the Father the promised Holy Spirit and has poured out from what you now see and hear. For David did not ascend to heaven, and yet said, 'The LORD to my Lord; sit at my right hand until I make

WHAT ARE WE FORGIVEN FROM?

your enemies a footstool for your feet.' Therefore let all of Israel be assured of this: God has made this Jesus whom you crucified both Lord and Messiah"

Hebrews 2:1-10: "We must pay the most careful attention, therefore, to what we have heard; so that we do not drift away. For since the message spoken through the angels was binding and every violation and disobedience received its just punishment, how shall we escape if we ignore so great a salvation? This salvation, which was first announced by the Lord, was confirmed to us by those who heard him. God also testified to it by signs and wonders and various miracles and gifts of the Holy Spirit distributed according to his will. It is not to angels that he subjected the world to come, about which we are speaking. But there is a place where someone has testified: 'What is mankind that you are mindful of them, a son of man that you care for him? You made them a little lower than the angels, you crowned them with glory and honor and put everything under their feet.' In putting everything under them, God left nothing that is not subject to them. But we do see Jesus, who was made lower than the angels for a little while, now crowned with glory and honor because he suffered death, so that by the grace of God he might taste death for everyone."

Ephesians 1:3-10: "Praise be to the God and Father of our Lord, Jesus Christ, who has blessed us in the heavenly realms with every spiritual blessing in Christ. For he chose us in him before the foundation of the world to be holy and blameless in his sight. In love, he predestined us for adoption through Jesus Christ, in accordance with his pleasure and will—to the praise of his glorious grace, which he has freely given us in the One he loves. In him we have redemption through his blood, the release from our sins, in accordance with the riches of God's love that he lavished on us. With all wisdom and understanding he made known to us the mystery of his will according to his good pleasure, which he purposed in Christ, to be put into effect when times reach their fulfillment to bring unity to all things in heaven and on earth under Christ."

Galatians 4:4-9: "And when the set time had fully come, God sent his Son born of a woman, born under the Law, to redeem those under the Law that we might receive adoption to sonship. Because you are his sons, God sent the Spirit of his Son into our hearts, the Spirit who calls out, 'Abba Father.' So you are no longer a slave, but God's child; and since you are his child he has also made you an heir." An heir is a person who is legally entitled to property or rank of another upon that person's death. The Son of God was made low that the Son of man be lifted up, Christ became a curse for us, for it is written: (Deuteronomy 21:23) "Cursed is everyone who is hung on a pole." And by his death he redeemed us. He legally gave his life that we could receive what is promised to us by making us his heirs. All the promises in the Word of God are for the believer. If you believe, I pray that today you take ahold of

WHAT ARE WE FORGIVEN FROM?

that which Christ Jesus took hold of for you.

> *"For I have been crucified with Christ and I no longer live, but Christ lives in me. This life I now live in the body, I live by faith in the Son of God, who loved me and gave himself up for me" (Galatians 2:20).*

PART 3
WHAT ABOUT GRACE?

Psalm 18:26: "To the pure you show yourself pure, but to the devious you show yourself shrewd."

Devious, what an interesting word. In the Oxford Dictionary, devious is defined as showing a skillful use of underhanded tactics to achieve goals. In other words, it means dishonest.

In John 5:39-40, Jesus says, "You study the Scriptures diligently because you think that in them you have eternal life. These are the very Scriptures that testify about me, yet you refuse to come to me to have life."

To those who are dishonest, God shows himself shrewd. If we have accepted that the Word of God is true and we are trying our best to live out what it says but we never come to Jesus to have life, then we are underhandedly trying to achieve a goal in our own strength. Is doing good your goal, or is knowing Him your goal? If the goal is to have life in Jesus, then we must come to Jesus in order to have life. Jesus is not works. Jesus is a person. He is the Son of God. It is only through Him that we have life. We can only come to Him by grace through faith. In James 2:17, it says, "In the same way, faith by itself, if it is not accompanied by action, is dead." Some might say that because they have the action, then that means they have faith. My question is: faith in what? Is your faith in yourself to do good works? Believing in yourself isn't faith. Faith only comes by grace and grace is a gift. Look at Ephesians 4:7: "However, he has given each one of us a special gift through the generosity of Christ." Wait, how does this gift come? It says through the generosity of Christ. Have you received the gift of grace through Christ's generosity? What is grace actually? Is it a free pass to sin and to get away with it? That is not what grace is at all. Grace has been taught many ways. It has been taught by people who cherish it and also by people who abuse it. That is just another reason why it is so necessary for you to read your Bible for yourself and to be still to listen and hear the voice of the Lord. When people understood that salvation is also a gift and that it cannot be earned, grace then became the hot topic of the pulpit. People agreed with what was right, and when they "slipped up," they claimed grace. Slip up, relapse, messed up are sugar coated words for un-surrendered. The gift of grace frees us from being slaves to sin. Grace isn't the means to keep you "out of hell," Grace is the means to walk in obedience to truth. You were created to have union with God. That union was broken when sin entered into mankind through the disobedience of one man. As a result, people try to line up their actions with moral code. Everyone is looking for acceptance because, until they come to the knowledge of truth, they will believe a lie. Satan is the father of lies. He will have people believe that God is mad at them because of their terrible actions. He will trick you to believe him. He will teach you things like false humility where you will take vows of poverty, remain defeated because you are just a no-good sinner that God had to come and save. God didn't save you so you could stay the same busted up sinner that you were before you met Him. God saved you from life apart from Him, which is what death is. It is complete separation from God. It is utter darkness. Hear me when I say this: God is not punishing you. He poured out your punishment on His very own Son. He poured out all of His wrath on His Son, Jesus. And when He did, Jesus said, "Father, forgive them for they know not what they do" (Luke 23:34). The only thing God wants to prove to you is that He loves you. But you will never know His love until you know His Son, Jesus. Grace is the generosity of Jesus Christ taking the punishment of death for the sin of mankind so that those who call upon His name can be set free from the punishment of being separated from God. Colossians 1:13 tells us that "He has rescued us from the dominion of darkness and brought us into the kingdom of the Son he loves, in who we have redemption, the forgiveness of sins." So we were born apart from him in the kingdom of darkness, and Jesus, who paid the penalty of this death, this separation from God, now holds the authority to free you from the enemy's camp, so to speak. True grace brings freedom. Misused grace brings arrogance against the Word of God and keeps you bound to lies. There will never be enough lies to comfort the one who denies Jesus as the Son of God. But those who want to know Him will forsake the notion of unbelief because of the desire in their heart to behold Him. Philippians 3:10: "I want to know Him—

yes, the power of His resurrection and participation in His sufferings, becoming like Him in His death, and so, somehow, attaining to the resurrection from the dead. Not that I have already obtained this, or have already arrived at my goal, but I press on to take hold of that for which Christ Jesus took hold of me."

AUTHOR'S PERSONAL TESTIMONY

Hi. My name is Talli Lopez. I first met Jesus at an early age through my parents. They truly lived out what they believed. To me, my childhood was perfect. It was not perfect because of us, but it was perfect because our family was rooted and grounded in love. Perfect is not really an action; it is a completion. And we were complete because we were in Christ. My whole life, people have commented on my smile and the joy that is evident in my life. In my crucial teenage years, the joy slowly faded as I became friends with the world and learned that not everyone knows this Jesus who I believed in. I became ashamed and hid my joy because it was offensive to people who had no joy or had self-proclaimed joy. People often told me that I thought I was "too good" because I didn't want to do the things they were doing. That was until I started doing the things they were doing. It was well into my twenties that I realized I had become just like the world who didn't know Jesus. My desire was always to please the Lord. But I did not understand that, because I lost connection with the Word of God as my authority, I was trying really hard to "be good" in my own strength. I even got married twice, not because I was in love but because I was desperately trying to do things right. The problem was that, no matter how hard I tried, I kept falling short and giving in. It was years of frustration as I indulged in alcohol and cigarettes. I was self-centered and self-focused, all while trying to create a successful and unforgettable childhood for my two innocent daughters. Through it all, God never left me. He never did. His hand has always been upon me and my children. He always took care of us. He always made a way where it seemed impossible. My children are worshippers. They don't worship on a platform, though they have. But they worship the Lord in Spirit and in truth. In fact, many times I would wake up hungover and hear my oldest daughter in her room singing praises to God and my youngest daughter in her room reading her Bible and praying. As a mom, this broke my heart in more ways than I could ever explain. I am here to tell you today that on November 24, 2019, God delivered me from alcohol and cigarettes. I have not had a drop since and live a life completely sober, grounded in truth. Little by little, all the things that held me back from being who God designed me to be have been removed from my life. Some are taking longer than others, but God is faithful! I can now say that this Jesus who I came to know through my parents many years ago is the same Jesus I now know for myself. He is even greater than I ever imagined. He is my Salvation, He is my hope, and He is my risen King. I will exalt Him. I am His. "For I am not ashamed of the Gospel, because it is the power of God that brings salvation to everyone who believes: first to the Jew, then to the Gentile" (Romans 1:16).

www.ingramcontent.com/pod-product-compliance
Lightning Source LLC
Chambersburg PA
CBHW071048170125
20531CB00043B/684